Hall of Fame
LATERAL THINKING
PUZZLES

Albatross Soup and Dozens of Other Classics

Paul Sloane & Des MacHale

PUZZLE
WRIGHT
PRESS

An imprint of Sterling
Publishing Co., Inc.
www.puzzlewright.com

Puzzlewright Press and the distinctive Puzzlewright Press logo are
registered trademarks of Sterling Publishing Co., Inc.

Library of Congress Cataloging-in-Publication Data Available

The puzzles in this book originally appeared in:
Captivating Lateral Thinking Puzzles © 2007 by Paul Sloane and Des MacHale
Challenging Lateral Thinking Puzzles © 1992 by Paul Sloane and Des MacHale
Colorful Lateral Thinking Puzzles © 2003 by Paul Sloane and Des MacHale
Cunning Lateral Thinking Puzzles © 2006 by Paul Sloane and Des MacHale
Great Lateral Thinking Puzzles © 1994 by Paul Sloane and Des MacHale
Improve Your Lateral Thinking © 1995 by Paul Sloane and Des MacHale
Ingenious Lateral Thinking Puzzles © 1998 by Paul Sloane and Des MacHale
Intriguing Lateral Thinking Puzzles © 1996 by Paul Sloane and Des MacHale
Lateral Thinking Puzzlers © 1991 by Paul Sloane
Outside-the-Box Lateral Thinking Puzzles © 2009 by Paul Sloane and Des MacHale
Outstanding Lateral Thinking Puzzles © 2005 by Paul Sloane and Des MacHale
Perplexing Lateral Thinking Puzzles © 1996 by Paul Sloane and Des MacHale
Sit & Solve Lateral Thinking Puzzles © 2003 by Paul Sloane and Des MacHale
Super Lateral Thinking Puzzles © 2000 by Paul Sloane and Des MacHale
Test Your Lateral Thinking IQ © 1994 by Paul Sloane
Tricky Lateral Thinking Puzzles © 1999 by Paul Sloane and Des MacHale

All images used under license from Shutterstock.com

2   4   6   8   10   9   7   5   3   1

Published by Sterling Publishing Co., Inc.
387 Park Avenue South, New York, NY 10016
© 2011 by Sterling Publishing Co., Inc.
Distributed in Canada by Sterling Publishing
c/o Canadian Manda Group, 165 Dufferin Street,
Toronto, Ontario, Canada M6K 3H6

Manufactured in the United States of America
All rights reserved

Sterling ISBN 978-1-4027-7117-0

For information about custom editions, special sales, premium and
corporate purchases, please contact Sterling Special Sales
Department at 800-805-5489 or specialsales@sterlingpublishing.com.

Acknowledgments

We would like to acknowledge the input and inspiration of many people, including those too numerous to mention by name from all over the world, who have written to us with ideas and encouragement. Also to the contributors to the Lateral Puzzles Forum (www.lateralpuzzles.com) who have given comments and feedback on some early ideas for this book.

This book could not have been produced without the help in editing and reviewing provided by Peter Gordon, Francis Heaney, Patrick Blindauer, and Jeffrey Harris. Also, special thanks to Craig Humphrey for "Here, Fido," Peter Bloxsom for "Dalí's Brother," Jean-Claude Franc for "Hosing Down," the Broughton family of Brecksville, Ohio, for "The Painter" and "Smart Appearance," Micheal O'Fiachra for "Shoe Shop Shuffle," Lloyd King for "Twin Peeks," Michael Humphrey for "Sick Leave," Felicia Nimue Ackerman for "No Thanks," Dan Crawford for "The Book," Bob Loper for "Mountains Ahead," Dee Bruder for "The Seven-Year Itch," Judy Dean for "The Elder Twin," and Kristen Stowe for "A Good Night's Sleep."

Contents

Introduction

If you have seen this kind of puzzle before, you will know that it consists of strange situations that require an explanation. They are designed as a form of game for a small group, where one person knows the answer and the others try to figure it out by asking questions. The questions can be answered only with "yes," "no," or "irrelevant." The puzzles can also be used as a form of training because they test and encourage skills in questioning, imagination, inductive reasoning, and lateral thinking.

Sure, some of the situations are implausible. And sure, it is possible to come up with alternative solutions that fit the original puzzle. In fact, you can play a variation of the game where people try to think of as many alternative explanations as possible. But in general, you will get the most enjoyment from these puzzles if you keep questioning until you come up with the answer given in the book. There is a clues section to help out when you get stuck, but the best resource is always your own imagination.

For this collection, we have assembled from our previous 16 books what we think are some of the greatest lateral thinking puzzles ever devised. We hope you think so, too.

—Paul Sloane and Des MacHale

The Puzzles

Fair Deal

Several truck drivers at a roadside café started to play poker. The pot was large and the game was serious. Suddenly one of the men accused the dealer of cheating. The dealer drew a knife and, in plain view of all the others, stabbed the man and killed him. The police were called and they interviewed everyone who had been present. But no man was arrested or charged with any offense. Why not?

Clues on p. 59/Answer on p. 92

Buck Up

A man is holding a bucket full of water. He turns the bucket upside down but the bucket remains full of water. How come? (Before you respond: the bucket has no lid, the water is not frozen, the man is not in a space capsule, and he is not swinging the bucket around so that centrifugal force keeps the water in the bucket.)

Clues on p. 59/Answer on p. 92

Glass Phobia?

Why did a woman smash all the light bulbs in her home?

Clues on p. 59/Answer on p. 92

Here, Fido

A man staying at a friend's house made a telephone call. Then he frantically ran around the house looking for the friend's dog. Why?

Clues on p. 59/Answer on p. 92

Postpaid

A man with two hobbies took great care to send a letter to an address which he knew did not exist. Why?

Clues on p. 59/Answer on p. 93

Time Out

A holy man sets out to climb a mountain up the only path at noon on Tuesday. He reaches the summit at midnight, prays, fasts, and then sleeps until noon on Wednesday. At noon he starts down the mountain path very slowly and carefully and reaches the bottom of the mountain at midnight. Can you show that there must be some time on the clock such that he was at the same point on the path going up on Tuesday and coming down on Wednesday at that time?

Clues on p. 59/Answer on p. 93

Crossings

Four people have to cross a narrow bridge in the dark. They have one flashlight between them, which must be used on the crossings. One or two can cross at a time but not more than two. One of them can cross in 1 minute, one in 2 minutes, one in 4 minutes, and one in 10 minutes. What is the shortest elapsed time for them all to cross the bridge?

Clues on p. 60/Answer on p. 93

The Fisherman

An avid fisherman lived near a large lake that contained many fine fish. He fished from his motorboat. He would travel all along his side of the lake in search of fish, but he would never go to the southeastern part of the lake, even though the fishing there was good and it was within easy reach of his boat. Why did he never go to that part of the lake?

Clues on p. 60/Answer on p. 93

The All-Night Party

In a small town in the United States a teenage boy asked his parents if he could go to a friend's party. His parents agreed, provided that he was back before sunrise. He left the house that evening clean-shaven and when he returned just before the following sunrise his parents were amazed to see that he had a fully grown beard. What happened?

Clues on p. 60/Answer on p. 93

The Postman

A postman had to deliver a letter to a house that was surrounded by a five-foot wall. The house could be approached only by the main path. Unfortunately, a ferocious dog was tied by a long leash to a tree nearby, so that the path was well within the dog's range. If the postman walked up the path, he was sure to be attacked by the dog. How did he outmaneuver the dog and deliver the letter?

Clues on p. 60/Answer on p. 94

The Unsuccessful Robbery

A gang of armed robbers burst into a large bank. They demanded all the money from the tills. The bank manager pointed out that there was none. They then insisted that he open the safe. He did so but there was no money inside. Just then the police arrived and arrested the gang. What was going on?

Clues on p. 60/Answer on p. 94

Cash in Hand

Smith had owed Jones a thousand dollars and, although Jones asked for the sum many times, Smith never repaid it. Then one day Smith offered to repay Jones the thousand dollars in cash, but Jones refused to accept it. Why?

Clues on p. 60/Answer on p. 95

Page 78

. . . .

Every week a woman went to the local library. If she saw a book that looked interesting, she immediately turned to page 78 before deciding whether she should borrow the book or not. Why?

Clues on p. 61/Answer on p. 95

Seven Bells

. . . .

A little shop in New York is called "The Seven Bells," yet it has eight bells hanging outside. Why?

Clues on p. 61/Answer on p. 95

The Accident

A careless driver caused an accident. Fortunately, both he and the driver of the other car were wearing seat belts and were uninjured. However, a passenger in the other car (who was not wearing a seat belt) was very badly mangled in the accident and lost both his legs as a result. When the case came to court the careless driver escaped with a small fine. Why was the judge so lenient?

Clues on p. 61/Answer on p. 95

Bus Stop

A woman travels by bus to a certain building every day. There are two bus stops on her side of the street. One is 100 yards before the building and the other is 200 yards beyond the building. She always gets off at the bus stop 200 yards past the building and walks back. Why?

Clues on p. 61/Answer on p. 95

Western Sunrise

We all know the sun rises every day in the east and sets in the west. One day, a man saw the sun rise in the west. How?

Clues on p. 61/Answer on p. 95

The Statue

A huge and heavy statue had to be lifted onto a large pedestal base in the middle of a town square. The bottom of the statue was completely flat and there was no way of lifting it except by putting ropes around and under it. How did they manage to get the ropes out from under the statue once it was lifted onto the base?

Clues on p. 62/Answer on p. 96

Assault and Battery

. . . .

John is guilty of no crime, but he is surrounded by professional people, one of whom hits him until he cries. Why?

Clues on p. 62/Answer on p. 96

Fair Fight

. . . .

A boxer left the ring after winning the national championship. His trainer took all the money and he never got a cent. Why not?

Clues on p. 62/Answer on p. 96

Once Too Often

. . . .

If you do it once, it's good. If you do it twice on the same day, though, it's a serious crime. What is it?

Clues on p. 62/Answer on p. 96

Chimney Problem

. . . .

An industrial archaeologist was examining an abandoned factory in a remote place with no one in sight or within earshot. He climbed to the top of an old 100-foot chimney by means of a rusty old ladder attached to the outside of the chimney. When he got to the top, the ladder fell away, leaving him stranded. How did he get down?

Clues on p. 62
Answer on p. 96

The Unbroken Arm

Why did a perfectly healthy young girl put a full plaster cast on her arm when it was not injured in any way?

Clues on p. 62/Answer on p.

Dalí's Brother

Some time after Salvador Dalí's death, his younger brother became famous as (believe it or not) a surrealist painter. This younger brother had great international success and the word "genius" was used to describe him. His name was Dalí and he did not change it. Yet today, the world remembers only one Dalí and few people even know that he had a brother. Why is this?

Clues on p. 63/Answer on p. 97

Bare Bones

During an examination, a medical student is handed a human femur (thigh bone). The examiner asks the student, "How many of these do you have?"

The student replies, "Five."

"Wrong," says the examiner, "You have two femurs."

But the student is right. How come?

Clues on p. 63
Answer on p. 97

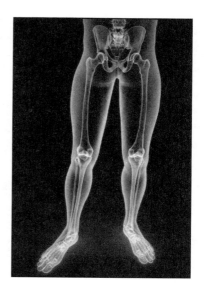

Poor Investment

Why did a company spend millions of dollars trying to find something that costs only a few thousand dollars?

Clues on p. 63/Answer on p. 97

The Wrong Ball

A golfer drove his ball out of sight over a hill. When he got there, he saw a ball that was the same make as his own and identical to it in every way. But he knew immediately that it was not his ball. How come?

Clues on p. 63/Answer on p. 97

Hosing Down

Because it was raining, the firemen hosed down the road. Why?

Clues on p. 63/Answer on p. 97

Secret Assignment

The famous physicist Ulam one day noticed that several of his best graduate students had disappeared from his university. They had in fact gone to Los Alamos to take part in the top-secret preparations for the first atomic bomb. They were sworn to secrecy. How did Ulam find out where they had gone?

Clues on p. 64/Answer on p. 97

Walking Backward

A man walked backward from the front door of his house to his kitchen. Someone rang the doorbell and the man ran quickly out of his back door. Why?

Clues on p. 64/Answer on p. 98

Free Lunch

A man in a restaurant used two forks and one knife. He did not pay for his lunch. What was happening?

Clues on p. 64/Answer on p. 98

Right Off

A man comes out of his house to find that his new car is damaged beyond repair after he has paid for it but before he has had time to insure it. However, he is absolutely delighted at what has happened. Why?

Clues on p. 64/Answer on p. 98

Ouch, That Hurts!

Why did a woman deliberately trap her hair in a window?

Clues on p. 64/Answer on p. 99

Two Lefts Don't Make a Right

A man leaves home, makes three left turns, and returns home without speaking to anyone. He is very pleased. Why?

Clues on p. 65/Answer on p. 99

Beginner's Luck

A man who was a poor and inexperienced poker player sat down to play poker with several other men who were all skilled and experienced players. The man won a lot of money. How?

Clues on p. 65/Answer on p. 99

Sure Thing
. . . .

You are challenged to play chess simultaneously by two inter-national chess grandmasters. You don't even know the rules of chess. You get two points for a win and one point for a draw. Can you think of a plan that will gain you at least two points?

Clues on p. 65/Answer on p. 99

Bostonian
. . . .

A man was born in Boston, Massachusetts. Both his parents were born in Boston, Massachusetts. He lived all his life in Boston but he was not a United States citizen. How come?

Clues on p. 65/Answer on p. 99

The Man in the Bar
. . . .

A man walked into a bar and asked the bartender for a glass of water. They had never met before. The bartender pulled a gun from under the counter and pointed it at the man. The man said "Thank you," and walked out. Why?

Clues on p. 65/Answer on p. 99

The Lumberjacks

Tim and Joe are two lumberjacks who work at the same rate of speed. One morning, Tim works steadily from 8 o'clock to noon without taking a break. Joe starts and finishes at the same times, but he takes a five-minute break every half-hour. At the end of the period Joe has felled considerably more trees than Tim. How come?

Clues on p. 65/Answer on p. 100

The Painter

Much of his painting was seen at the city's two large art galleries but no one had ever heard of him. Why not?

Clues on p. 66/Answer on p. 100

Pay Phone

A lady depended on a public pay phone to make calls but it was frequently out of order. Each day she reported the problem to the telephone company but nothing was done. Finally she phoned the company with a false piece of information that caused the telephone to be fixed within hours. What did she tell them?

Clues on p. 66/Answer on p. 100

Library Lunacy

A public library suddenly announced that each member could borrow up to ten books and not return them for up to six months. Why?

Clues on p. 66/Answer on p. 100

Smart Appearance

Victor was smartly dressed, well shaven, and with the best haircut he'd had for years. Many of his friends and relatives saw him, yet no one complimented him. Why not?

Clues on p. 66/Answer on p. 100

Two Suitcases

A man is carrying two suitcases, one in each hand. One is a big empty suitcase. The other is a smaller light suitcase full of books. He puts the smaller suitcase into the bigger one, making it heavy and difficult to carry. Why does he do this?

Clues on p. 66/Answer on p. 100

The Two Drivers

Two drivers drove slowly and safely in the correct direction down a wide road before coming to a stop in front of a red stop light. A nearby police officer immediately arrested one of the drivers and let the other one drive off. The police officer had never seen nor heard of either driver before. Neither driver had a criminal record. They were both fully dressed and no one had been drinking. Both cars were in excellent roadworthy condition and had not been stolen. The arrested driver was charged and convicted. Of what?

Clues on p. 66/Answer on p. 100

Keys in the Car

A man locks his keys inside his car and is unable to get them out despite trying for an hour. A police officer comes along and offers to help. He discovers that the back door of the car is unlocked and he consequently recovers the keys. The man thanks him, but when the officer departs the man locks the back door, leaving the keys inside. Why?

Clues on p. 67/Answer on p. 100

Time of Arrival

A teenage boy returned home from a party very late and silently crept upstairs to his bedroom. No one saw or heard him arrive. The next morning when his mother asked him what time he had arrived home, he replied, "About one o'clock." How did she know that he had, in fact, arrived much later?

Clues on p. 67/Answer on p. 101

The Parcel

Why did a lady deliberately leave a parcel behind when she got off the bus?

Clues on p. 67/Answer on p. 101

Sitting Ducks

Why does a woman with no interest in hunting buy a gun for shooting ducks?

Clues on p. 67/Answer on p. 101

Trunk-ated

The police stop a car and they suspect that the trunk contains evidence linking the driver with a serious crime. However, they do not have a search warrant and if they open the trunk forcibly without probable cause, any evidence uncovered will not be admissible in court. How do they proceed?

Clues on p. 67/Answer on p. 101

Wonderful Walk

A man and his dog went for a walk in the woods. When he returned home he invented something now worth millions of dollars. What was it?

Clues on p. 67/Answer on p. 102

Shoe Shop Shuffle

In a small town there are four shoe shops of about the same size, each carrying more or less the same line in shoes. Yet one shop loses three times as many shoes to theft as each of the other shops. Why?

Clues on p. 68/Answer on p. 102

Hot Picture

A woman paid an artist a large sum to create a picture, and she was very pleased with the results. Yet within a week, under her instructions, the picture was burned. Why?

Clues on p. 68/Answer on p. 102

The Burial Chamber

Why did a man build a beautiful burial chamber, complete with sculptures and paintings, and then deliberately wreck it?

Clues on p. 68/Answer on p. 102

Miscarriage of Justice

A Roman judge released a guilty man and convicted an innocent man and as a result the confectionery industry has greatly benefited. Why?

Clues on p. 68/Answer on p. 102

Psychic

You enter a parking lot and see a woman walking toward you. You then see a row of cars and know immediately which one is hers. How?

Clues on p. 69x/Answer on p. 103

Poor Show

Every time he performed in public, it was a complete flop. Yet he became famous for it, and won medals and prizes. People came from all over and paid to see him perform. Who was he?

Clues on p. 69/Answer on p. 103

The World's Most Expensive Car

The most expensive car ever made is for sale. Although many people want to own it and can afford to buy it, nobody will do so. Why?

Clues on p. 69/Answer on p. 103

The Stranger in the Bar

Two men went out for a drink together in a bar. One of them looked up, saw a tall, dark stranger looking like death and drinking soda, and pointed him out to his companion. Startled and uneasy, the two men left and went to another bar some miles away. After a few minutes, they looked up and saw the same sad, pale stranger drinking soda. Deciding to leave, they went to a third bar, which was empty except for a young couple. However, within a few minutes, the cadaverous man appeared and, in a slow, sad voice, ordered a soda. Almost out of his mind, one of the men went over to him and said, "Who are you and what do you want?" What did the man answer?

Clues on p. 69/Answer on p. 104

The Cabbie's Revenge

An American tourist in London took a taxi cab. When he reached his destination, the tourist paid the taxi driver the fare, but did not include a tip. The taxi driver was displeased and said something to the American that ruined his whole evening. The two men were strangers and had never met previously. What did the cabbie say?

Clues on p. 70/Answer on p. 104

Bad Impression

A man entered a city art gallery and did terrible damage to some very valuable Impressionist paintings. Later that day, instead of being arrested, he was thanked by the curator of the art gallery for his actions. How come?

Clues on p. 70/Answer on p. 104

Light Work

There are three light switches outside a room. They are connected to three incandescent light bulbs inside the room. Each switch can be in the on position or the off position. You are allowed to set the switches and then to enter the room once. You then have to determine which switch is connected to which bulb. How do you do it?

Clues on p. 70/Answer on p. 104

The Coconut Millionaire

A man buys coconuts at $5 a dozen and sells them at $3 a dozen. As a result of this he becomes a millionaire. How come?

Clues on p. 70/Answer on p. 104

Mona Lisa

Why did a group of enterprising thieves steal the famous painting known as *Mona Lisa* and then return it undamaged a few months later?

Clues on p. 70/Answer on p. 105

The Wounded Soldier

. . . .

A badly wounded but conscious soldier is brought into a field hospital during a battle. The surgeon takes a quick look at him and then says to the orderly, "Get this man out of here! He is a coward who has smeared himself with the blood of his comrades." Why did he say this?

Clues on p. 71/Answer on p. 105

Rich Man, Poor Man

. . . .

A man making over $10 million a year drives a small car, lives in a modest house, and insists he can't afford luxuries. Why not?

Clues on p. 71/Answer on p. 105

The Hairdresser

. . . .

A New York City hairdresser recently said that he would rather cut the hair of three Canadians than one New Yorker. Why?

Clues on p. 71/Answer on p. 105

The King

. . . .

A man is crowned king. Shortly afterwards, he is captured by enemy forces and pulled apart. Why?

Clues on p. 71/Answer on p. 105

Twin Peeks

Jasmine's two best friends, Josh and Phoenix, are twins and always look identical—they even wear matching clothes. While walking to school Jasmine noticed one of the twins walking ahead of her. Not knowing whether it was Josh or Phoenix, she called out, "Hi there." As soon as he turned to face her she knew it was Phoenix. How did she know?

Clues on p. 71/Answer on p. 106

Dampened Spirits

Why did a man deliberately wet his pants?

Clues on p. 71/Answer on p. 106

Back Again

A man working in an office is fired from his job. Why does he show up at the office early the next morning?

Clues on p. 72/Answer on p. 106

Nervous Wreck

A ship sank in 20-foot-deep water, blocking the entrance to a harbor. All efforts to raise it failed until a sports shop owner came up with an idea that did the trick. What did he suggest?

Clues on p. 72/Answer on p. 106

Singles

Why did one member of a band insist on being paid in single dollar bills only?

Clues on p. 72/Answer on p. 106

Fly by Night

Traditionally it is not allowed for the U.S. flag to be hung at full staff outdoors at night, except in one place. Where?

Clues on p. 72/Answer on p. 106

Hide and Seek

A spy is tipped off that the police will raid and search his house the next morning to find and confiscate his secret codebook. There is nobody he trusts enough to give it to, so where does he hide it for safekeeping?

Clues on p. 72/Answer on p. 107

The Odd Shot

At a major golf tournament, a player's ball is in the rough. He has a clear view of the pin on the green, but he does not play his shot towards the green. He opts to chip out on to the fairway instead. Why?

Clues on p. 73/Answer on p. 107

Rival Arrival

Antonia was hosting a high society ball. She heard that her social rival, Gwendoline, was planning to wear the same ball gown as Antonia. What did she do to upstage her foe?

Clues on p. 73/Answer on p. 108

The Inventive Survivor

A man was in a hotel room when a terrible fire broke out. He was trapped in his room on the 20th floor and the window did not open. Poisonous smoke was coming under the door and through the air conditioning system. He started to choke. If he could last another 10 minutes help would arrive. What did he do?

Clues on p. 73/Answer on p. 108

The Driverless Car

On a dark and rainy night a hitchhiker was having no luck finding a ride. Finally a car stopped and he got in. But something was very odd—there was no driver! Suddenly the car started moving. The hitchhiker saw a curve coming up and reached for the steering wheel but a hand came through the window and turned the car. The ride continued, and each time a curve came, the hand reached in and turned the car just in time. Finally the car stopped and the hitchhiker ran into a bar, ordered a large Scotch, and told everyone what had just happened. Then two men came up to him. What did they say?

Clues on p. 73/Answer on p. 108

Stand and Deliver

. . . .

A man and his wife were sitting comfortably having a drink. Suddenly they both stood up and lifted their hands in the air. Why?

Clues on p. 74/Answer on p. 108

Spaced Out

. . . .

The Americans spent several million dollars developing a certain space technology. The Russians achieved the same technology for virtually nothing. What was it?

Clues on p. 74/Answer on p. 108

Cube Root

. . . .

Why did a woman put two cubes in a glass of water?

Clues on p. 74/Answer on p. 109

Tap on the Shoulder

. . . .

A passenger in a taxi tapped the driver on the shoulder to ask him something. The driver screamed, lost control of the cab, nearly hit a bus, drove over the curb, and stopped just inches from a large plate glass window. What was the driver's explanation?

Clues on p. 74/Answer on p. 109

Undelicious

. . . .

A man and his wife have dinner in an expensive restaurant. The food is first-class, the kitchen is spotless, the waitstaff is scrupulously clean, and the couple are not served any food to which they are allergic. Yet just after the meal both the man and his wife are violently ill. How come?

Clues on p. 74/Answer on p. 109

Lost and Found

. . . .

A man was driving alone in his car listening to his favorite cassette when he accidentally ejected it from its slot onto the floor of the car, which was already littered with used audio tapes. Without taking his eyes off the road he rummaged under his seat, picked up the correct tape, and reinserted it. How did he manage that?

Clues on p. 75/Answer on p. 109

Unlightable

A man is trying to light a fire. The sun is shining brightly and there is not a cloud in the sky. He is focusing the rays of the sun with a magnifying glass on some dry paper on the dry ground. Yet he fails to light the fire. Why?

Clues on p. 75/Answer on p. 110

Moldy Old Dough

Why did a baker deliberately add an ingredient to his bread that would make it go moldy in three days?

Clues on p. 75/Answer on p. 110

Sick Leave

Walter spent three days in the hospital. He was neither sick nor injured, but when it was time to leave he had to be carried out. Why?

Clues on p. 75/Answer on p. 110

Wonderful Weather

A ship sank in perfect weather conditions. If the weather had been worse, the ship would probably not have sunk. What happened?

Clues on p. 75/Answer on p. 111

Jericho

A man was building a house when it collapsed all around him. He wasn't injured or upset, and he calmly started to rebuild it. What was going on?

Clues on p. 76/Answer on p. 111

Absolute Madness

Why were 20 sane people put into a mental hospital?

Clues on p. 76/Answer on p. 111

Paper Tiger

A man writes the same number, and nothing else, on 20 sheets of paper. Why?

Clues on p. 76/Answer on p. 111

High on a Hill

A man was marooned overnight on a mountain above the snow line in winter. He had no protective clothing and no tent. How did he survive?

Clues on p. 76/Answer on p. 112

The Office Job

A man applied for a job in an office. When he arrived at the busy, noisy office he was told by the receptionist to fill out a form and then wait until called. He completed the form and then sat and waited along with four other candidates who arrived earlier. After a few minutes, he got up and went into an inner office and was subsequently given the job. The other candidates who had arrived earlier were angry. The manager explained why the man had been given the job. What was the reason?

Clues on p. 76/Answer on p. 112

The Upset Bird Watcher

A keen ornithologist saw a rare bird that he had never seen before, except in illustrations. However, he was very upset. Then he was frightened. Why?

Clues on p. 77/Answer on p. 112

Damage Control

During World War II, U.S. forces lost many bombers in raids over Germany due to antiaircraft fire. From the damage on returning bombers, they were able to build up a clear picture of which parts of the planes were hit most frequently and which weren't hit at all. How did they use this information to reduce losses?

Clues on p. 77/Answer on p. 113

School's Out

Why does an elderly lady receive a court order to go to school immediately?

Clues on p. 77/Answer on p. 113

The Single Word

A woman whom I had never met before was introduced to me. I didn't say a word. She told me about herself, but I didn't say a word. She told me many more things about herself, but I didn't say a word. Eventually I said one word and she was very disappointed. What was the word?

Clues on p. 77/Answer on p. 113

Turned Off

A man inadvertently caused all radio station transmissions in the world to cease. How? And who was he?

Clues on p. 78/Answer on p. 113

The Last Mail

A man mailed two letters to the same address at the same time in the same post office. The letters were identical but the postage on one letter was more than on the other. Why?

Clues on p. 78/Answer on p. 113

The Frame Game

Why did the curator of an art gallery remove a valuable painting from its frame?

Clues on p. 78/Answer on p. 114

Overdressed

It was a very warm day but George was wearing two suits, two shirts, two pairs of socks, an overcoat, and a hat. Why?

Clues on p. 78/Answer on p. 114

The Knifing

A masked man plunged a knife into Sam's chest. Sam was in a very serious condition and nearly died. When he recovered he tracked down the masked man and thanked him. Why?

Clues on p. 79/Answer on p. 114

Who's at the Door?

If Marjorie visited anyone on Saturday or Sunday she would ring the doorbell. If she visited anyone on a weekday, she would knock on the door. Why?

Clues on p. 79/Answer on p. 115

Airport Visitor

A man drives to the airport every day but never catches a plane. He does not work at the airport and he is not interested in airplanes. What is he doing?

Clues on p. 79/Answer on p. 115

Hanging Out

Why did a woman take a load of very wet laundry down from her clothesline and replace it with perfectly dry clothing?

Clues on p. 79/Answer on p. 115

No Thanks

A disabled man was offered a good job by a reputable university. Why did he turn it down?

Clues on p. 79/Answer on p. 115

Dotty

Why do drive-in banks have Braille on their automatic teller machines?

Clues on p. 80/Answer on p. 115

Your Turn to Drive

Two brothers were talking. One said, "I am fed up with living in Birmingham because I have to drive all the time. Why don't we move to London?" His brother replied, "But that would mean that I would have to drive all the time." Why is this true?

Clues on p. 80/Answer on p. 116

Coming Up for Air

As part of a school experiment a girl was sent to the middle of a nearby city with instructions to collect a sample so that pollution levels could be measured. She was given a glass container with a removable but tight-fitting lid. Of course, she realized that the jar contained comparatively clean air from the school environment. How did she ensure that she excluded this air and retrieved an absolutely accurate sample of the city air?

Clues on p. 80/Answer on p. 116

Nuts Away!

A man was changing a wheel on his car when the four nuts used to hold the wheel in place fell into a sewer drain and were lost. He was afraid he was stuck there, but a passing boy made a very useful suggestion that enabled the man to drive off. What was the boy's idea?

Clues on p. 80/Answer on p. 116

The Golf Pro

Although there are very few golf tour professionals who are left-handed, most clubs prefer to have left-handed golf pros as instructors. Why?

Clues on p. 81/Answer on p. 116

Flat Tire

Four college students arrived late for a lecture, explaining to their instructor that their car had suffered a flat tire on the way there. How did the clever lecturer immediately show those assembled that the late arrivals were not telling the truth?

Clues on p. 81/Answer on p. 117

Bottled Fruit

We all know there's a way to get a ship into a bottle. How would you get a full-sized pear into a bottle without damaging the pear or breaking or cutting the bottle?

Clues on p. 81/Answer on p. 117

The Village Idiot

. . . .

Visitors to a scenic mountain village were often amused by the village idiot. When offered a choice between a shiny 50-cent piece and a crumpled $5 bill, he would always happily choose the half-dollar. The bill was worth ten times as much, so why did he never choose it?

Clues on p. 81/Answer on p. 117

Hand in Glove

. . . .

A French glove manufacturer received an order for 5,000 pairs of expensive sealskin gloves from a New York department store. He then learned that there was a very expensive tax on the import of sealskin gloves into the United States. How did he (legitimately) get the gloves into the country without paying the import tax?

Clues on p. 82/Answer on p. 117

The Fallen Sign

. . . .

A man was walking in country unfamiliar to him. He came to a crossroads where he found that the signpost showing various town names and the distances to them had fallen over. How did he find out which way to go?

Clues on p. 82/Answer on p. 117

The Cellar Door

. . . .

A little girl was warned by her parents never to open the cellar door or she would see things that she was not meant to see. One day while her parents were out she did open the cellar door. What did she see?

Clues on p. 82/Answer on p. 118

The Lake Problem

There is a large irregularly shaped lake on your estate. It is of variable and unknown depth. There are no rivers or streams entering or leaving the lake. How would you find the volume of water in the lake?

Clues on p. 83/Answer on p. 119

Albatross Soup

Two men went into a restaurant. They both ordered albatross soup. After they tasted it one of the men immediately got up from the table, went outside the restaurant, and shot himself. Why?

Clues on p. 83/Answer on p. 119

Traffic Offense

A man goes to work in the same manner every working day for 20 years. However, one morning going to work in the same way, he is ticketed by the police. Why?

Clues on p. 83/Answer on p. 119

Meeting and Greeting

A woman was hurrying down a street when she met an old friend she had not seen for many years. She did not shake hands or wave to her friend. Why not?

Clues on p. 83/Answer on p. 119

Garment for Rent

Why did a man destroy the sweater that his wife had made for him?

Clues on p. 84/Answer on p. 119

Bad Loser

A man playing in the final round of a tough competition loses. In a fit of anger, he shoots the winner with a gun with the result that his opponent can never play again. However, the police are not called, and the man escapes with a fine and a simple warning. Why?

Clues on p. 84/Answer on p. 119

Unsanitary Janitor

Why did the janitor dip his mop in the toilet before cleaning the bathroom mirror?

Clues on p. 84/Answer on p. 120

The Man in the Elevator
. . . .

A man lives on the tenth floor of a building. Every day, he takes the elevator to the first floor to go to work or to go shopping. When he returns, he always takes the elevator to the seventh floor and then walks the remaining flights of stairs to his apartment on the tenth floor. Why does he do this?

Clues on p. 84/Answer on p. 120

The Men in the Hotel
. . . .

Mr. Smith and Mr. Jones are two businessmen checked into the same hotel for the night. They are given adjacent rooms on the third floor. During the night, Mr. Smith sleeps soundly. However, despite being very tired, Mr. Jones cannot fall asleep. He eventually phones Mr. Smith and falls asleep immediately after hanging up. Why?

Clues on p. 85/Answer on p. 121

Happy or Sad
. . . .

Three women dressed in swimsuits were standing together. Two were sad and one was happy. But the sad women were both smiling and the happy one was crying. Why?

Clues on p. 85/Answer on p. 121

Trouble With Sons
. . . .

A woman had two sons who were born in the same hour of the same day in the same year, but they were not twins. How could this be so?

Clues on p. 85/Answer on p. 121

The Miller's Daughter

Many years ago, there was a poor miller who could not afford to pay the rent on his mill. His greedy old landlord threatened to evict him, his wife, and his daughter. However, the landlord did offer an option. If the miller's beautiful young daughter would marry the old man, then he would forget their debts and let the miller and his wife live in the mill rent-free.

The family met to discuss this proposition. The daughter was horrified at the prospect of marriage to the old man, but she realized that it might be the only hope for her parents. She suggested a compromise. They would draw lots. If the landlord won, she would meet his request, and if she won, he would wipe out all debts without her having to marry him. The landlord agreed.

The two stood on a stony path that had many black and white pebbles. The landlord suggested that they put one black pebble and one white one in a bag. She would have to draw a pebble from the bag. If it were black, she must marry him, and if it were white, she would be free. She reluctantly agreed to this suggestion. He bent down and picked up two pebbles to put in the bag, but she noticed that he had cheated and put in two black pebbles.

She could expose him by showing that there were now two black pebbles in the bag, but he would lose so much face in front of all the people that he would be very angry and probably evict them. How could she seem to go along with the plan and yet triumph, knowing that there were two black pebbles in the bag?

Clues on p. 85/Answer on p. 121

Water and Wine

There are two glasses on the table, one containing water and the other one wine. They both contain exactly the same amount by volume. If you take a teaspoon of water and mix it into the wine and then take a teaspoonful from the wine glass and mix it with the water, both glasses become contaminated. But which is the more contaminated? Does the water now contain more wine than the wine does water, or is it the other way around?

Clues on p. 85/Answer on p. 121

Old Mrs. Jackson

Mr. and Mrs. Jones were young and active people. Their next-door neighbor, Mrs. Jackson, was a 93-year-old invalid. One day, they asked her into their house to do something that neither of them could do. There was no skill that she had that one of them did not have, so why did they need her help?

Clues on p. 86/Answer on p. 122

Stuck Tight

A truck became wedged under a low bridge. It could not move forward or back without severely damaging its roof. The truck driver was perplexed until a little girl standing nearby suggested an easy solution. What was it?

Clues on p. 86/Answer on p. 122

Coming Home

A man walked home after having been out drinking. He walked down the middle of a deserted country road. There were no street lights to illuminate the road and there was no moonlight. He was dressed all in black. Suddenly a car that did not have its headlights on came racing down the road. At the last moment, the driver of the car saw the man and swerved to avoid him. How did he manage to see him?

Clues on p. 86/Answer on p. 122

Push That Car

A man pushing his car stopped outside a hotel. As soon as he got there, he knew he was bankrupt. Why?

Clues on p. 86/Answer on p. 122

Woman on the Bridge

During World War II, there was a footbridge over a ravine between Germany and Switzerland. It was guarded by a German sentry. His orders were to shoot anyone trying to escape over the bridge and to turn back anyone who did not have a signed authorization to cross. The sentry was on the German side of the bridge. He sat in a sentry post and he came out every three minutes to survey the bridge.

There was a woman who desperately needed to escape from Germany to Switzerland. She could not possibly get a pass. She knew that she could sneak past the sentry while he was in the sentry post, but it would take between five and six minutes to cross the bridge. There was no place to hide on or under the bridge, so the guard would be easily able to shoot her if he saw her on the bridge escaping to Switzerland. How did she escape across that bridge?

Clues on p. 87/Answer on p. 122

School Friend

Joe went back to his hometown and met an old school friend he had not seen for years. His friend said, "I am married now but not to anyone you know. This is my daughter."

Joe turned to the little girl and asked her her name. She said, "I have the same name as my mother."

"Then you must be called Louise," said Joe. He was right, but how did he know?

Clues on p. 87/Answer on p. 122

The Two Barbers

A traveler came to a small town in the middle of nowhere. He had never visited it before, he knew no one there, and he knew nothing about the town or its inhabitants.

He needed a haircut. There happened to be two barber shops close to each other on the main thoroughfare—the only barber shops in town. The man studied each of them with care. One shop was very neat and tidy. Everything about it was smart. The barber was sweeping away the last traces of hair from the floor while waiting for his next customer.

The other barber's shop was very untidy. Everything looked rather run down and ramshackle. The scruffy-looking barber within was lolling on a chair waiting for his next customer.

Both shops charged the same amount for a haircut. After careful consideration, the traveler decided to go to the scruffy barber for his haircut. Why?

Clues on p. 87/Answer on p. 123

The Plane Hijacker

A young man hijacked a passenger flight at gunpoint. He ordered the pilot to fly to a different airport and radioed his demands to the airport authorities. In return for the safe release of the plane and hostages, he asked for $100,000 in a bag and two parachutes. When the plane landed, he was given the bag of money and the two parachutes. He then instructed the pilot to take off again and to fly at a fairly low altitude toward their original destination. When they were over a deserted part of the country, he strapped on one of the parachutes and, clutching the bag of money, leapt from the plane. The second parachute was not used.

He was never found. The task of the police was to find that hijacker. Your task is different. You only have to answer one question: Why did he ask for two parachutes if we assume that he only ever intended to use one?

Clues on p. 87/Answer on p. 123

The Hunter and the Bear

There was a hunter who started out from his camp one morning. He walked one mile due south and then saw a bear. He followed it eastward for exactly one mile, at which point he shot it. He then dragged it northward for one mile to the same camp that he had started from. What color was the bear?

Clues on p. 88/Answer on p. 124

The Arm of the Postal Service

One day a man received a parcel in the post. Inside, he found a human left arm. He examined it carefully and then repacked it and sent it on to another man. The second man also examined the arm. He then took it out to the woods and buried it. Why would they have done these things?

Clues on p. 88/Answer on p. 124

The Book

A woman walked up to a man behind a counter and handed him a book. He looked at it and said, "That will be four dollars." She paid the man and then walked out without the book. He saw her leave without it but did not call her back. How come?

Clues on p. 88/Answer on p. 125

Mountains Ahead

. . . .

You are seated next to the pilot of a small plane that is one mile above sea level. Huge mountains loom directly ahead. The pilot does not change speed, direction, or elevation, yet you survive. How come?

Clues on p. 88/Answer on p. 125

River Problem

. . . .

A man came to a river carrying a fox, a duck, and a bag of corn. There was a boat in which he could ferry one of the three items across the river at any one time. He could not leave the fox alone with the duck, nor the duck alone with the corn, so how did he get all three across?

Clues on p. 89/Answer on p. 125

The Seven-Year Itch

. . . .

While digging a garden, a woman unearthed a large metal box filled with money and jewelry. For seven years she spent none of the money and told no one what she had found. Then she suddenly bought a new house, a new car, and a fur coat. How come?

Clues on p. 89/Answer on p. 125

The Follower
. . . .

A woman who was driving on her own pulled into a gas station and bought some gasoline. As she drove off, she noticed a stranger in a car following her. She tried to shake him off by turning, accelerating, slowing down, etc. Finally she turned into a police station, but she was shocked to see him follow her in. He was not a policeman and there were no mechanical faults with her car. Why did he follow her?

Clues on p. 89/Answer on p. 126

The Dog Choker
. . . .

A woman came home to find her dog choking in the hall. She rushed the dog to a nearby vet and went home while he examined the dog. When she arrived home the phone was ringing. It was the vet warning her to get out of the house at once. Why?

Clues on p. 89/Answer on p. 126

The Elder Twin
. . . .

One day, it was Kerry's birthday. Two days *later*, it was the birthday of her *older* twin brother, Terry. How come?

Clues on p. 89/Answer on p. 126

The Key
. . . .

Every night before he went to bed, a man carefully locked all the doors of his house. Then he placed the front-door key inside a bucket of cold water. In the morning he retrieved the key from the bucket in order to open the door. Why did he do this?

Clues on p. 90/Answer on p. 127

A Good Night's Sleep

. . . .

A man in a hotel was unable to sleep. He got up, opened the window drapes, went back to bed, and fell asleep easily. How come?

Clues on p. 90/Answer on p. 127

A Puzzling Attack

. . . .

Four rational and reasonable people were seated around a table. Suddenly three of them jumped up and viciously beat the fourth one senseless. Why?

Clues on p. 90/Answer on p. 127

The Clues

Fair Deal

- There was nothing faked or pretended about this incident. The dealer had murdered the man who was stabbed.
- The dealer was punished for the crime.

Buck Up

- No fountains or pressurized water systems are involved.
- The man got wet.

Glass Phobia?

- What do light bulbs do? This scenario might sound familiar to some moviegoers.

Here, Fido

- Who/where could he have called?
- What purpose could finding his friend's dog serve?
- He wanted information.

Postpaid

- The man was a collector and a music fan.
- He cleverly combined his two interests to achieve a very collectible item.
- He knew that his letter would not be delivered and would be returned.

Time Out

- He might have walked at different speeds on the two days or paused at different points.
- Try thinking of his progress as a chart or a graph.
- What if there were more people doing this on the same day?

Crossings

- There is no catch here. Simple logic will get you the solution.
- Two people go over and one comes back (bringing the flashlight) on the first few crossings.
- There are two slower people. How can you minimize the time that it takes them both to cross?

The Fisherman

- His reluctance to go to the far side of the lake has nothing to do with fishing.
- There is no physical barrier across the lake. However, the fisherman is acting rationally in not going there. There is a danger to the fisherman in crossing to the other side of the lake.
- Other people do cross the lake safely. Under certain circumstances the fisherman could also cross safely. He would need to get permission.

The All-Night Party

- No potions, transplants, wigs, or tricks were involved. It was the same boy and he returned before the next sunrise, having been out long enough to grow a proper beard.

The Postman

- He did not use anything to distract the dog except himself.

The Unsuccessful Robbery

- Their timing was very poor.
- The bank had had plenty of money at the start of the day.

Cash in Hand

- Smith offered to pay Jones the thousand dollars at a time when it would have been disadvantageous for Jones to accept it.
- Whichever of them had the money would lose it shortly.

Page 78

- She was not looking for a particular book, but for books in general that were interesting and new.

- Her husband read the books.

Seven Bells

- The shopkeeper could easily change the sign, but chooses not to do so.

- No superstition about numbers is involved.

- Many people notice the discrepancy.

The Accident

- The driver's car was white. The other car was black.

Bus Stop

- The woman does not meet anybody or pass anything of interest or benefit to her by going to the farther bus stop. She does not like exercise.

- When the woman comes home, she walks to the nearer bus stop in order to catch the bus.

- The woman finds it easier to walk 200 yards from the far bus stop, rather than 100 yards from the near bus stop.

Western Sunrise

- No mirrors or reflections are involved. The man saw the celestial sun rise in front of him in the west.

- He was on the planet Earth, not in a spaceship, or in space, or at the North or South Pole.

- Looking west, the man first saw the sun set, then a little later he saw it slowly rise again.

The Statue

- No ramps, slides, or levers were used. The statue was not tilted or dropped.

- The statue was lowered using ropes. The ropes were removed. The statue then settled very slowly onto the base.

Assault and Battery

- John is healthy.

- The person who hits John does it to help him.

- It is a common occurrence.

Fair Fight

- The boxer did not expect to collect any money.

- The trainer collected a worthwhile sum for his efforts.

- The boxer won fairly, but without throwing a punch.

Once Too Often

- You can do this many times in your life.

- You do it on a specific day that is not of your choosing.

- It is variously considered a right, a privilege, and a duty.

Chimney Problem

- He came down very slowly.

- The chimney was not the same after he finished his descent.

The Unbroken Arm

- She was not seeking sympathy or help. Nothing was concealed in the cast.

- She was about to do something important.

- She knew that the plaster cast would be noticed immediately.

Dalí's Brother

- Salvador Dalí is recognized as a brilliant surrealist painter.
- Salvador Dalí's younger brother was actually a brilliant surrealist painter but his older brother never knew this.
- The two brothers had something important and unusual in common.

Bare Bones

- The student was healthy and was not physically abnormal.
- She had never had any kind of medical operation.
- Every human is born with two femurs.

Poor Investment

- They could easily buy another of these items; in fact, they had several spare ones.
- If it was lost, then it had to be found.
- They were looking for information.

The Wrong Ball

- The ball was clearly visible and accessible.
- He did not touch the ball or examine it. He knew it wasn't his immediately upon seeing it.

Hosing Down

- They used regular water. The road was not contaminated in any way.
- It was for a special event.
- They did not hose the entire road.

Secret Assignment

- Knowing the students' habits, he did some clever detective work.
- He knew they were serious and studious, and always prepared themselves for assignments.
- He checked something in a particular place at the university.

Walking Backward

- There was no one else in the house.
- The man was not afraid of any danger to himself.
- He did not know who had rung the bell.
- He ran out the back in order to run around to the front of the house.

Free Lunch

- The man ate his lunch with one knife and one fork.
- He provided a service.
- The restaurant provided an intimate atmosphere in the evenings.

Right Off

- He is upset that his new car is ruined, but pleased at something else.
- No other vehicle is involved.
- He acquires something rare.

Ouch, That Hurts!

- She trapped the hair on her head—not cut hair.
- She was alone at the time. No one else was involved.
- She did it for reasons of safety.

Two Lefts Don't Make a Right

- He knows as soon as he leaves home that he has achieved his objective.
- He wears a uniform.
- Home is not a house.

Beginner's Luck

- The man had no special powers or abilities that helped him at playing cards.
- The other men suffered from no disadvantages or disabilities that prevented their playing well.
- The man had never met the other players before but he had been invited to join their game.

Sure Thing

- You are given a choice of colors: white or black in each game.
- You are happy to lose one game if you can win the other.
- The games are played in adjacent rooms, and you can wander from game to game as you wish.

Bostonian

- There was nothing strange or unusual about this man.
- His friends and neighbors in Boston were also not U.S. citizens.

The Man in the Bar

- The bartender was not expecting any kind of message or messenger.
- The man was not expecting the bartender to pull a gun.
- The man said "Thank you" because he was grateful.
- The bartender was normal, but the man had an ailment of sorts.

The Lumberjacks

- During his breaks, Joe does something that helps him to cut more trees.

The Painter

- He was a very good painter whose work could be seen at art galleries and private houses.

- He was not shy of publicity and he used his own name.

- He did not paint on canvas.

Pay Phone

- She gave the telephone company a strong incentive to fix the pay phone.

- She told the telephone company that some people were very pleased that the telephone did not work properly.

Library Lunacy

- The library benefited from this temporary change in the rules.

- This relaxation of the normal rules of borrowing was a one-time event caused by something else that was happening at the library.

Smart Appearance

- Professional help had been involved in making Victor look particularly dapper.

- Everyone noticed how dapper he looked but no one spoke to him.

Two Suitcases

- He does not intend to carry the suitcase far.

- He is trying to save money.

The Two Drivers

- Although the two drivers had driven in identical fashion, one had committed an offense and the other had not. The police officer acted properly.

- It happened in a hot country.

Keys in the Car

- The man did not mean to lock his keys in the car. He had no criminal or ulterior motive. It was an accident.

- When he had been unable to retrieve his keys, the man had initiated another course of action in order to get them.

Time of Arrival

- The mother deduced correctly from what she saw that he must have arrived in very late.

- When he came in, the boy did not make a sound. He removed his shoes and then crept up to bed.

The Parcel

- It was something that she made for someone else.

- She knew it would probably be found and handed in.

Sitting Ducks

- The woman loves animals and hates hunting. She does not intend to use the gun for hunting or for self-defense.

- There is no criminal intent in mind.

- The ducks are already dead when she shoots them.

Trunk-ated

- The policeman is able to prove that there is something suspicious in the trunk without opening it.

- He suspects that there is a body in the trunk.

- How do you attempt to contact a dead man?

Wonderful Walk

- Something annoying happened during the walk in the woods.

- It gave the man an idea.

- He invented a popular fastener.

Shoe Shop Shuffle

- The four shops have similar staffing, lighting, and security arrangements.
- The shop that suffers the heaviest thefts is not in a worse part of town or in an environment that is more popular with criminals.
- The shop that suffers the heaviest thefts does something different with its shoes.

Hot Picture

- She loved the picture, but she deliberately had it burned. No trace of it was left.
- There was no criminal intent on her part, and she did not make any financial gains.
- The picture was a present.
- Her husband was a motorcyclist.

The Burial Chamber

- The burial chamber wasn't built for use by the builder.
- No one was buried there when he wrecked it.
- He did not wreck it out of spite or anger. He deliberately destroyed it in order to deceive.
- He wrecked the chamber for purposes of preservation.

Miscarriage of Justice

- The Roman judge tried a rebel, but released a robber.
- The Roman was not in Rome when he made the judgment.
- The judge, the rebel, and the robber never ate any chocolate.

Psychic

- You see the cars after you see the woman, and you did not see her leaving her car.
- There is something different in the appearance of her car.
- She is carrying something.

Poor Show

- His performances were always a flop, but he was very successful.
- He did not work in comedy, music, cinema, or theater.
- His most famous performance was in Mexico.
- He was a sportsman.

The World's Most Expensive Car

- The car was used once and is in good condition, but it has not been driven for many years.
- Many people have seen it on TV, but they can't name the man who drove it.
- It was developed at great expense for practical use and not for show or exhibition.

The Stranger in the Bar

- The two men were drinking beer while the stranger was drinking soda.
- The two men hadn't noticed the stranger outside the bars, but there was a connection between them and the stranger.

The Cabbie's Revenge

- The cabbie did not insult the American. He did not make any personal or nationalistic comment.

- The cabbie gave the American a piece of factual information that the American did not want to hear. (We cannot tell you exactly what the cabbie said because it might ruin an evening for you, too!)

- The location to which the American was driven by the cabbie is important.

Bad Impression

- He deliberately sprayed water over the paintings. This damaged them.

- He was not unstable, deranged, or malevolent. He acted out of good intentions.

Light Work

- With just two bulbs and two switches, it would be easy.

- Light bulbs give out light. What else do they do when they are switched on?

The Coconut Millionaire

- He lost money on every coconut he sold.

- He did not make money by any activity related to the coconut sales.

Mona Lisa

- They did it for money.

- No insurance payment was involved. The thieves did not receive any reward or payment from the police, museum, insurance company, or any public body.

The Wounded Soldier

- The soldier was genuinely wounded and was not a coward. The surgeon knew this.

- The surgeon lied, but had good intentions and wanted to help the soldier.

Rich Man, Poor Man

- The man makes over $10 million a year at his work but he does not have a lot to spend.

- He is not wealthy, nor does he have any major debts or expenses.

The Hairdresser

- The New York hairdresser had nothing against New Yorkers and has no particular love of Canadians.

- He charges everyone the same price for one haircut.

The King

- Twelve men started out in the attempt to become king. The one who succeeded was one of the few to survive.

Twin Peeks

- Jasmine deduced correctly that it was Phoenix in front of her. But there was nothing in his appearance to distinguish him from his twin brother.

- She knew because he turned around.

Dampened Spirits

- It was an emergency, but fire was not involved.

- His action helped him to escape.

- It was cold, but he did not need to thaw anything.

Back Again

- The man did not forget anything or have any incomplete work-related business to take care of.

- He was not angry or upset.

- He was dismissed from his job for just cause and he was now out of work.

- His former place of work now served a new purpose for him.

Nervous Wreck

- The ship had been empty but was now full of water.

- The ship was positioned in such a way that hoists and cranes would not work. An inflatable float was suggested but not used; it would have been cut by sharp edges caused by the wreck.

Singles

- He did it to ensure that he was not cheated.

- The musician later became a world-famous singer and pianist.

Fly by Night

- Generally, someone should bring the flag down and take it in at the end of the day.

- There is one place where it is not possible to do this.

Hide and Seek

- The spy found a clever way to ensure that the codebook was not found during the police search.

- The police searched the house very thoroughly.

- It is a method that any of us could use if we knew that our premises were due to be searched on a certain day.

The Odd Shot

- The player wants to win the competition, but he deliberately takes a more difficult route to the hole knowing that it will almost certainly cost him a shot.

- The player is not trying to gain an unfair advantage—quite the opposite.

- This is his first shot of the day.

Rival Arrival

- Antonia did not want to be seen in the same dress that someone else was wearing.

- Gwendoline arrived in the dress.

- No other guest wore the dress but Gwendoline was still very upset.

The Inventive Survivor

- He found a source of air but he did not break any walls or windows.

- He did not have air tanks or unusual equipment of any kind.

- He survived by going into the bathroom, even though smoke was pouring into the bathroom.

The Driverless Car

- What happened was not a prank.

- The car was real.

- The car moved very slowly.

Stand and Deliver

- It was not a hold-up. They were not in danger.

- They were not applauding or exercising.

- They were watching a sporting event.

- They were not trying to attract someone's attention.

Spaced Out

- It was a piece of communications equipment.

- It allowed astronauts to record information under zero gravity conditions.

- Both the Russians and the Americans already had something that would do the job.

Cube Root

- The cubes are not ice cubes or sugar cubes.

- No drink or refreshment is involved.

- Dropping the cubes in the water could save her a lot of money.

Tap on the Shoulder

- The driver was reacting to the tap on the shoulder.

- After the passenger got in and gave his destination, nothing was said between them.

- The driver had only recently become a taxi driver.

Undelicious

- Some other people who ate at the same restaurant were also ill.

- There was nothing wrong with the food or drink in the restaurant.

- If they had had the same meal in the same restaurant on the previous night they would have been fine.

Lost and Found

- All the tapes were the same size and shape.
- He had listened to most of the tracks on the tape.
- He could tell which one he needed by feeling it.

Unlightable

- There is nothing unusual about the paper.
- There is no wind, rain, humidity, or other weather condition that would make it difficult to light a fire.
- He focuses the sun's rays accurately and they heat up the paper to a temperature at which it would normally ignite.

Moldy Old Dough

- He did not do this to sell more bread nor for any financial gain.
- He did this so that the bread would not last more than three days.
- This happened in Australia in the 19th century.

Sick Leave

- Walter was human and physically normal.
- The hospital was a normal hospital.
- He wasn't able to walk into the hospital or out of it.

Wonderful Weather

- The accident happened at night.
- No other craft was involved.

Jericho

- Although he constructed it with great care, the man thought that the house might fall down.
- He didn't intend that he or anyone else live in the house.

Absolute Madness

- They were received into the hospital as insane.
- They had not carried out any action to indicate that they were insane.
- They hadn't met before, but there was a link between them.
- They had all set out to travel by bus.

Paper Tiger

- The sheets of paper were important. He wrote the numbers in ink.
- He intended to keep the papers for his later personal use.
- He did this each year at a certain time of year.

High on a Hill

- The man managed to stay warm but he didn't burn anything.
- The man was alone. No person or animal heped him to keep warm.
- The mountain was dangerous.

The Office Job

- The man's age, appearance, gender, and dress didn't matter.
- Everyone had completed the form correctly and in a similar fashion.
- The man showed that he had a skill required for the job.

The Upset Bird Watcher

- The bird was just as beautiful and rare as he had imagined. He wasn't disappointed with its appearance.

- What happened to the bird placed him at risk.

- He saw the bird through a small window.

Damage Control

- Some damage is fatal to a plane and some is not.

- The returning planes are not a true sample of all the planes and all the damage.

- U.S. bomber command used the information about damage on returning planes to strengthen planes and so reduce losses.

School's Out

- She was instructed to go to school for her education.

- She was already very old (and well educated).

- She was issued the court order automatically.

The Single Word

- Other people also heard what she had to say.

- There is no sexual connotation to the story. The narrator could be male or female.

- The word I said summarized a decision that would significantly affect the woman.

- None of my companions was allowed to speak in the woman's presence.

Turned Off

- The man didn't interfere with the physical operation of the radio stations.

- There was no threat or misinformation.

- All radio stations voluntarily chose to stop transmitting for a short period.

The Last Mail

- There was no difference in the contents, envelope, or addressing of the two letters.

- They were both sent by the same method—first class.

- The same clerk at the same post office handled both letters.

- The man weighed the letters and found their weights were identical. He then put stamps on them and took them to the postal clerk, who told him that one of the letters was fine but that the other needed more stamps.

The Frame Game

- He did his for security purposes with all the valuable paintings in the museum.

- He made a small mark on the painting where it could not normally be seen.

Overdressed

- He was indoors and very uncomfortable.

- He did not do it to change his appearance or as part of a bet or a game.

- He did it to save money.

The Knifing

- The masked man deliberately stabbed Sam. This was no accident.

- The man wore a mask over his face—but not to hide his identity.

- Prompt medical attention saved Sam's life.

Who's at the Door?

- Marjorie works on weekdays, and her job is relevant.

- She chooses to knock for safety reasons.

- Ringing the bell could be dangerous.

Airport Visitor

- The man stands in line at check-in but he never checks in.

- He profits from his behavior.

- He is a criminal.

Hanging Out

- The woman is married, but her husband wasn't home at the time.

- He was able to see the clothesline, however.

No Thanks

- The man had a visible medical condition that affected the upper half of his body.

- The school was a well-known American university, the position he was offered was one he'd been looking for, and the university's facilities had no drawbacks as far as he was concerned.

- He turned the job down when he heard the name of the university.

Dotty

- The ATM makers do not make Braille panels with the intent that they should be used at drive-in banks.

- There is no legal requirement to feature Braille on the drive-in machines. The banks do it for economic reasons.

Your Turn to Drive

- Both brothers were able and licensed to drive.

- One always drove in Birmingham and the other always drove in London.

- This was due to necessity, not a personal choice. They did not like this.

- When one brother drove, the other was a passenger.

- Their jobs are irrelevant, but the cities are relevant.

- The brothers were not completely normal.

Coming Up for Air

- She could not get a valid sample by simply taking the lid off the jar and shaking it around; she could not be sure that she had removed all of the original air.

- She did not use a machine to create a vacuum.

- The solution involved no advanced physics or complicated devices. She used a very simple idea.

Nuts Away!

- The boy suggested a way of attaching the wheel.

- It did not involve retrieving the lost nuts.

- It did not involve any equipment not normally available in a car.

- It was a sensible idea that was easy to implement.

The Golf Pro

- It has nothing to do with a left-hander's golf clubs, equipment, or methods.

- It is because left-handed players make better teachers, but why is that so?

Flat Tire

- The instructor could not tell from their clothing or any other external factor whether they were telling the truth.

- The tardy students had in fact arrived by car but had suffered no puncture or flat tire.

- The lecturer asked them one question, which exposed their deceit.

Bottled Fruit

- This is not only physically possible, but it is often done. Some producers sell a fully grown pear inside each bottle of pear liqueur.

- No special implements or aids are used.

- The bottle is not formed around the pear.

The Village Idiot

- The village idiot was not a complete idiot.

- There was a good reason for him to always choose the coin rather than the bill.

- Getting the money in coin form was somehow more useful for him than getting it in bill form would be.

Hand in Glove

- The glove manufacturer did not smuggle the gloves into the country. He was a reputable businessman.

- He did not disguise the gloves as something else.

- He did not end up paying any duty.

- Goods are impounded if you refuse to pay duty, and are then sold at auction to the highest bidder. The value of the sets of gloves at auction would be higher than the duty.

The Fallen Sign

- The man could not determine the correct position by matching the broken parts of the post or the post with the hole in the ground.

- He did not use the sun, stars, wind, or a landmark as a guide.

- He used a piece of knowledge to replace the sign correctly in the ground.

- Anyone could have done the same; it required no special skill or knowledge.

The Cellar Door

- What the little girl saw amazed and surprised her.

- It would not amaze or surprise most people, though.

- Something unusual was kept in the cellar, but that's not what she saw.

- She did not see a living creature.

The Lake Problem

- The solution does not involve measuring the height of the water in the lake.

- The solution does not involve measuring the temperature of the lake.

- The solution is a practical and realistic way of estimating the volume of water in the lake.

- The solution involves taking samples of water from the lake.

Albatross Soup

- The soup was not poisoned, and it was not distasteful to anyone but the man who shot himself.

- Tasting the soup caused the man to deliberately commit suicide.

- The man shot himself because he did not recognize the taste.

- The man had done something previously that caused him to believe that he would recognize the taste.

Traffic Offense

- He drives to work.

- Something had changed, but it was more fundamental than just a traffic light.

- How had he forgotten after all that publicity?

Meeting and Greeting

- The woman would normally have shaken hands with her friend, but today she was not able to.

- She was rushing today, but her hurry was not the only reason that she did not shake hands with her friend.

- She was rushing to the hospital.

- She had suffered a serious accident.

Garment for Rent

- By destroying the sweater, he saved his life.
- The sweater was never a danger to him.
- He put the sweater to another use.

Bad Loser

- The loser used a real gun with real bullets with the intention of harming his opponent.
- The man and his opponent were competing against each other to win a prize.
- The man was playing a board game.

The Unsanitary Janitor

- The janitor was following instructions.
- Although what he did was unhygienic, he did it with worthy motives.
- He worked at a school.
- His action was designed to improve behavior.

The Man in the Elevator

- He doesn't do anything between the seventh and tenth floors besides climb stairs.
- If someone else was with him, they would both take the elevator to the tenth floor.
- If he lived on the sixth floor, he would go up to the sixth floor in the elevator.
- If he lived in a different apartment in a different country, but still lived on the tenth floor, he would probably do the same thing he does now.

The Men in the Hotel

- Something was happening in Mr. Smith's room that prevented Mr. Jones from sleeping.

- There was a noise coming from Mr. Smith's room.

- They did not speak for long on the phone.

Happy or Sad

- They were not at a beach or a swimming pool.

- It is relevant that they were wearing swimsuits.

- They were beautiful, shapely women.

- The happy one was crying because she was happy.

- The sad ones were not smiling because they were sad.

Trouble With Sons

- The two boys are brothers, born of the same father and mother on the same day of the same year at the same place.

The Miller's Daughter

- Think of a way whereby she could use the fact that she knows she will draw a black pebble to give a result that would indicate a white pebble.

- Remember that a double negative is a positive.

Water and Wine

- Remember that after the two transfers each glass contains the same volume that it started with and the same volume as the other glass.

Old Mrs. Jackson

- Mrs. Jackson performed a physical action for the Joneses.

- It was not something that they could do or learn to do for themselves.

- Mrs. Jackson would have been able to perform the same service for another couple.

Stuck Tight

- The bridge and the truck were normal.

- The road could not be lowered, and the bridge could not be raised.

- The girl's idea was easy to implement and involved no special equipment.

Coming Home

- The man was not carrying a flashlight or any other illumination.

- There was no starlight or lightning.

- The driver saw the man.

- Anyone could have seen the man.

Push That Car

- The man had to push the car.

- The car could never be driven.

- The hotel was on a famous road.

- He was bankrupt because he had to pay money to the hotel owner.

Woman on the Bridge

- She did not escape by running over the bridge or hiding in it.
- She escaped by tricking the guard in some way.
- The guard followed his orders.

School Friend

- Joe did not know who had married his friend. He had no other source of information than this conversation.
- He knew that the girl's mother was named Louise.

The Two Barbers

- The man was making a considered and rational choice in going to the scruffy barber.
- His choice was governed solely on the desire to get a good haircut.
- He made the right decision.
- He had seen examples of each barber's work.

The Plane Hijacker

- The man did not change his mind during the course of the hijack. He always intended to leap out of the plane on his own.
- He did not carefully choose one of the parachutes in preference to the other.
- He asked for two parachutes to deceive the airport authorities.
- He did this to protect himself.

The Hunter and the Bear

- If you go one mile south, then one mile east, and then one mile north, you usually finish approximately one mile west of where you started. The distance is not exact because the Earth is spherical.

- This is not the case at the North Pole. However there are other places on Earth where this is possible.

The Arm of the Postal Service

- Each of the two men only had one arm.

- The man who sent the parcel only had one arm.

- The sender willingly amputated his own arm before sending it through the mail.

- All three had been present when the first two had lost their arms, but they did not lose their arms via an accident.

The Book

- He was not surprised that she left without the book.

- She did not pay the money to buy the book.

- She received nothing in return when she gave him the money, but she was quite happy to pay it.

Mountains Ahead

- The pilot has control of the aircraft.

- There is no tunnel, hole, or other way through the mountains.

- You were never in serious danger.

- You did not fly over, around, or past the mountains.

River Problem

- Play around with the possibilities; you will soon arrive at the answer.

The Seven-Year Itch

- The woman did not wait in order to avoid observation by the police or criminals.

- The money and jewelry was stolen, but this is irrelevant.

- She would have liked to spend the money earlier.

- She was somehow physically prevented from spending the money.

- She was not in prison.

The Follower

- He was not a danger to her.

- He was trying to help her.

- He had not seen anything wrong with her car.

The Dog Choker

- The dog was a guard dog.

- The vet had not found evidence of poison or gas.

- The vet deduced that there was a danger in the house.

- The vet discovered what the dog was choking on.

The Elder Twin

- Kerry and Terry were genuine human twins, born of the same mother of the same pregnancy.

- Terry, the older twin, was born before Kerry.

- Her birthday was always before his.

- The locations of the births matter.

The Key

- It was a regular man in a regular house with a regular key.
- He did not put the key in the bucket to prevent another person or creature from getting it.
- This does not involve criminal intent or the prevention of criminal action.
- He did this to protect the safety of his wife.
- He did this to safeguard against a likely accident.

A Good Night's Sleep

- It was a normal hotel.
- The drapes were normal curtains, used to exclude light from coming through the window.
- No sound or light was stopping him from getting to sleep.
- There was something abnormal about the man.
- It was nighttime. No one else was involved.

A Puzzling Attack

- None of the four were criminals.
- The three had a very sound reason for beating up the fourth.
- He had said something that inflamed them.
- No little people, board games, or cellar doors were involved.

The Answers

Fair Deal

The police arrested the dealer and charged her with murder.

Buck Up

He is underwater.

Glass Phobia?

The woman is blind and is being pursued by a murderer. In the dark, he will be at a disadvantage if he cannot switch on lights. (From the 1967 movie *Wait Until Dark*.)

Here, Fido

The man had phoned an airline to arrange a flight. They said they would call him back and asked for his phone number. He did not know his friend's number but knew it was on the tag on the dog's collar, so he chased the dog to get it.

Postpaid

The man was a stamp collector and Elvis Presley fan. The U.S. Post Office issued a special Elvis stamp, so the man sent it to a fictitious address. It was returned marked "Return to Sender," the title of one of Elvis's greatest hits.

Time Out

Yes. Imagine the holy man starting his climb up and his identical twin starting his descent at the same time. There must be a point where the two of them cross.

Crossings

Let's call the four people 1, 2, 4, and 10, denoting how long it takes them to cross. This is the best sequence:

    1) 1 and 2 cross
    2) 2 returns
    3) 4 and 10 cross
    4) 1 returns
    5) 1 and 2 cross

The total elapsed time of the crossing is 17 minutes.

The Fisherman

A national border ran across the lake. The southeastern part of the lake was in another country, which was considerably more repressive and unfriendly than the homeland of the fisherman. Anyone crossing the border without all the necessary prior authorization was considered a spy and would be shot by the border guards.

The All-Night Party

The small town was Barrow in Alaska, the northernmost town in the United States. When the sun sets there in the middle of November, it does not rise again for 65 days. That allowed plenty of time for the boy to grow a beard before the next sunrise.

The Postman

The postman walked around the outside of the wall. The dog followed him, gradually winding its leash around the tree. The effective length of the leash was eventually reduced so much that the dog could no longer reach the path, so the postman delivered the mail.

The Unsuccessful Robbery

The gang had arrived at the bank shortly after another gang had robbed the bank.

Cash in Hand

Smith and Jones were traveling on the subway when a gang of muggers came into the car and started to take everyone's money. Smith offered to repay his debt to Jones just before the robbers reached them.

Page 78

The woman was borrowing books for her disabled husband who was confined to the house and a voracious reader. She could not remember which books he had already read, so they had a scheme. Whenever he read a book, or if she brought back a book he did not like, he made a small pencil mark at the bottom of page 78. She could then tell which books to avoid.

Seven Bells

It was originally a mistake, but the shopkeeper found that so many people came into his shop to point out the error that it increased his business.

The Accident

The other car was a hearse, and the passenger was already dead.

Bus Stop

The road on which the building stands is on a steep hill. The woman prefers to go past the building and walk down the hill, rather than get off earlier and walk up the hill.

Western Sunrise

He was the pilot of the Concorde. It took off shortly after sunset and flew west. It, therefore, caught up with the sun and the pilot saw the sun rise in front of him—in the west.

The Statue

Blocks of ice were placed on the pedestal so that the ropes on the bottom of the statue fitted between them. The ropes were then withdrawn. As the ice melted, the statue was lowered until it lay firmly on the base.

Assault and Battery

John is a newborn baby. The doctor slaps him to make him cry and use his lungs.

Fair Fight

The boxer was a dog that had just won the championship at a dog show.

Once Too Often

Voting twice in the same election is electoral fraud—a serious offense.

Chimney Problem

The man on the tall chimney had a penknife in his pocket. With this he pried loose a brick from the top layer. He used the brick as a hammer. In this way, he gradually demolished the chimney by knocking out all the bricks and lowered himself to the ground.

The Unbroken Arm

The healthy young girl put a cast on her arm before going to take a French oral examination. She figured (correctly) that the examiner would ask her about her injury. She came to the exam prepared with answers about how she broke it.

Dalí's Brother

Salvador Dalí died at age 2. Nine months later his brother was born and was also named Salvador. It was the younger Salvador Dalí who became the famous surrealist painter.

Bare Bones

The student was pregnant. She had two femurs of her own, two of her unborn baby, and one in her hands.

Poor Investment

The object is the black box flight recorder from a crashed jetliner.

The Wrong Ball

It had been a cold night and the ball was lying in a small frozen puddle.

Hosing Down

This incident occurred just before the start of the Monaco Grand Prix race, which is held in the streets of Monte Carlo. Part of the course runs through a tunnel. When it rains outside, the firemen hose down the road in the tunnel in order to make the surface wet. This improves consistency and safety.

Secret Assignment

Ulam went to the university library and examined the library records of all the books borrowed by the students over the previous month. Los Alamos was a common link to nearly all of them.

Walking Backward

The man walked backward from the front door as he varnished the wooden floor. He left the front door open for ventilation. When someone rang the doorbell, he quickly ran around to the front of the house in order to stop the person from walking inside onto the wet varnish.

Free Lunch

The man was a piano tuner who had come to tune the piano in the restaurant. He brought his own tuning fork. The restaurateur repaid the service with a free lunch.

Right Off

The car had been struck and destroyed by a large meteorite that the man found lying next to the car. The meteorite was rare and it was bought by a museum for over one million dollars.

Ouch, That Hurts!

The woman was driving her car alone at night. She felt drowsy and was concerned about falling asleep at the wheel. She trapped the ends of her long hair in the window. There was no discomfort if she kept her head up, but if she nodded off and her head slumped, the painful tug on her hair would wake her up.

Two Lefts Don't Make a Right

He is a baseball player who has just hit a home run.

Beginner's Luck

The man was a politician who had been bribed by several unscrupulous businessmen into giving them planning permission for a lucrative development contract. The problem was how to pay him without arousing suspicion. They invited him to play poker with them, and then deliberately lost. If they drew a good hand they folded, and if they had a weak hand they bet heavily against him. There is no law saying you must try hard to win at poker, so they were able to transfer the money to him under cover of the card game.

Sure Thing

If you play black in one game and white in the other, then you can effectively have one grandmaster play the other. Let one grandmaster make a move and then copy it to the other board. When your second opponent makes his reply, you use that move in the first game, and so on.

Bostonian

He was born in Boston, Massachusetts, in the early eighteenth century when it was still a British colony. He was British.

The Man in the Bar

The man had hiccups. The bartender recognized this from his speech and drew the gun to give the man a shock. It worked and cured the hiccups, so the man was grateful.

The Lumberjacks

Joe uses his breaks to sharpen his axe.

The Painter

He had painted the walls at the art galleries.

Pay Phone

She told the telephone company that people were making free international telephone calls because of a fault in the pay phone. They promptly sent an engineer to fix it.

Library Lunacy

The library was moving to new premises but had very little money for the move. By giving the borrowers extra time, it ensured that more of the books would be moved by borrowers and fewer by the movers.

Smart Appearance

The mortuary had prepared Victor well for his funeral.

Two Suitcases

The big suitcase is for bringing gifts back to his family. The man is on his way to check baggage at the airport, and now he only has to pay for one item.

The Two Drivers

This incident took place in Saudi Arabia in 1995. It is illegal for women to drive in Saudi Arabia. One driver was a man and the other a woman. The police officer arrested the woman, who was charged and convicted.

Keys in the Car

The man had already phoned his wife, who was 100 miles away, and persuaded her to drive to him with the spare set of keys. She had already traveled over halfway there, so he didn't want to have to explain to her that her journey was unnecessary and face her wrath.

Time of Arrival

When he came in, the boy had removed his shoes and placed them on top of the morning paper.

The Parcel

The parcel contained her husband's sandwiches, which he had forgotten to take to work. He worked in the lost and found office of the bus company.

Sitting Ducks

The woman is an aeronautics engineer. She uses the gun to shoot ducks at airplane engines to test how they handle high-speed impacts with birds.

Trunk-ated

A policeman suspects that there is the body of a murdered man in the trunk. He dials the cell phone of the victim and the phone is heard ringing in the trunk.

Wonderful Walk

During his walk in the woods, the man picked up several burrs on his clothes. When he returned home, he examined them under his microscope and discovered the mechanism whereby they stick on. He went on to invent Velcro.

Shoe Shop Shuffle

One shop puts left shoes outside as samples; the other three shops put right shoes out. Display shoes are stolen, but the thieves have to form pairs, so more are taken from the store showing left shoes.

Hot Picture

The woman commissioned a tattoo artist to produce a beautiful tattoo on her husband's back as a birthday present. The picture was fine, but the next day the unfortunate man was killed in a motorcycle accident. He was cremated.

The Burial Chamber

The man was building the burial chamber of an Egyptian pharaoh in ancient times. He built the real burial chamber deep inside a pyramid. He also built another burial chamber that was easier to find that he deliberately wrecked so that when any future graverobbers found it, they would think that earlier graverobbers had found the tomb and taken the treasure.

Miscarriage of Justice

The Roman was Pontius Pilate, who released Barabbas and condemned Jesus Christ to die by crucifixion at Easter time. Every year Easter is marked by the sale of millions of chocolate Easter eggs worldwide.

Psychic

You notice that the woman is carrying a kettle. It is a very cold morning and only one of the cars has the windshield deiced. You deduce correctly that she has defrosted her windshield with the kettle and is returning it to her home before setting off on her journey.

Poor Show

His name was Dick Fosbury, inventor of the famous Fosbury flop, a new high-jumping technique that involved going over the bar backward and that revolutionized the sport. He won the gold medal in the Mexico City Olympics in 1968.

The World's Most Expensive Car

The most expensive car was the moon buggy used by astronauts to explore the moon. It was left there. Even if NASA wanted to sell it, no one could retrieve it.

The Stranger in the Bar

He said, "I am the car service driver who has been driving you from bar to bar!"

The Cabbie's Revenge

The American was going to a performance of the famous Agatha Christie play *The Mousetrap*. The taxi dropped him outside the theater. The spiteful taxi driver said "X did it," where X was the name of the murderer in the play. (We cannot state here X's name or we might ruin your future enjoyment of the play!)

Bad Impression

He was a firefighter who, in the course of putting out a fire, sprayed the room and paintings with water. He had indeed damaged the paintings, but saved them and others from complete destruction.

Light Work

You set switches A and B on and switch C off. You wait a few minutes and then switch B off. You then enter the room. The bulb that is on is connected to A. The cold bulb that is off is connected to C. The warm bulb that is off is connected to B.

The Coconut Millionaire

The man was a philanthropist who bought great quantities of coconuts to sell to poor people at prices they could afford. He started out as a billionaire, but lost so much money in his good works that he became a millionaire!

Mona Lisa

The thieves handed the *Mona Lisa* back but not before they sold a dozen fake copies to gullible art collectors, each of whom believed he was buying the original. None of the buyers could go to the police because they were guilty of buying goods they believed to be stolen. By returning the original the thieves ensured that they would get only a light punishment if they were caught.

The Wounded Soldier

The surgeon had run out of life-saving adrenaline. He knew that the soldier was badly wounded and hoped to provoke a rush of natural adrenaline through the soldier's reaction to his false accusation.

Rich Man, Poor Man

He works at the mint. He makes many millions of dollars a year but draws a modest salary.

The Hairdresser

He gets three times as much money!

The King

This is normal in a game of checkers (or draughts).

Twin Peeks

Josh is deaf.

Dampened Spirits

The man was trapped in an avalanche. When pressed on all sides by snow you can easily lose your sense of direction. Some people burrow downward to escape and perish. Wetting his pants showed him the direction in which liquid flows, which is always downward, so he knew which way was up. (This is actually a piece of advice in some skiing manuals.)

Back Again

The man who lost his job had been working in the unemployment office. The next morning he showed up at the office looking for a new job.

Nervous Wreck

Tens of thousands of Ping-Pong balls were forced into the hold to displace the water. The ship then rose to the surface.

Singles

In the 1950s Ray Charles was just starting out on his musical career. He was a pianist in a band. When they were paid, since he was blind, he insisted on single dollar bills so that he could count exactly what he had received. Later, of course, he became a big star and a millionaire.

Fly by Night

On the moon.

Hide and Seek

Very early in the morning he mailed the codebook to his own address. It was delivered safely the day after the police search failed to find it.

The Odd Shot

The day before, the golfer was about to play a shot where a tree was blocking his view of the green, when an alert sounded to say there was danger of a thunderstorm and play was being suspended for the day. So he marked his ball. That night a huge bolt of lightning struck the tree and destroyed it. The next day, when he replaced his ball, he now had a clear view of the green but sportingly refused to take advantage of his good fortune and played the ball sideways onto the fairway as he intended to do originally.

Rival Arrival

Antonia wore a different dress and instructed her elderly maid to wear the original dress.

The Inventive Survivor

The shower head had a flexible hose; the man took it and pushed it through the water in the toilet basin. He breathed the air that was in the pipe beyond. The smoke did not pass through the water barrier.

The Driverless Car

The men said, "Are you the man who got into our car while we were pushing it?"

Stand and Deliver

They were in a stadium watching a sporting event. The crowd started doing "the wave," and they felt obliged to join in.

Spaced Out

The Americans invented a special ballpoint pen that worked under zero gravity conditions in space. The Russians used pencils.

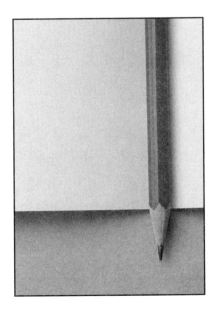

Cube Root

The cubes are a pair of dice to be used in a craps game. If they are loaded, they will always float to the bottom of the glass with their heaviest side down. This is a way of checking that the dice are fair.

Tap on the Shoulder

The driver explained to his worried passenger, "I'm sorry, it's really not your fault. Today is my first day driving a cab. I've been driving a hearse for the last 25 years!"

Undelicious

The restaurant was on board a ship, and they became seasick.

Lost and Found

The correct tape was warmer because it had been playing in the machine.

Unlightable

The man is an astronaut making an appearance on a kids' TV show. He is demonstrating that lighting a fire on the moon is impossible since there's not enough oxygen.

Moldy Old Dough

This happened in Tasmania in a penal colony in the 19th century. Prisoners trying to escape into the huge wilderness that surrounded the prison would often hoard their daily bread ration to survive the journey. Making the bread go moldy quickly ensured that the bread would become inedible quickly enough that prisoners would not have enough food with which to escape.

Sick Leave

Walter was a newborn baby.

Wonderful Weather

The ship was the *Titanic*, which hit an iceberg on a fine night when the sea was very flat. If the weather had been worse, then the lookouts would have seen waves hitting the iceberg or heard the iceberg. (Icebergs make groaning noises when they move.) Unfortunately the iceberg wasn't seen in time and the rest is history.

Jericho

The man was building a house of cards.

Absolute Madness

A bus driver was told to bring 20 psychiatric patients to a mental hospital. On the way he stopped to buy a newspaper. When he got back, all his passengers had gone. So he drove up to several bus stops and collected the first 20 passengers he could find and delivered them to the hospital, where he warned the staff that they would all cause trouble and claim to be sane.

Paper Tiger

It's January and he is writing the date of the year on all the checks in his checkbook to avoid putting last year's date by mistake.

High on a Hill

The man was marooned on a volcano that had recently erupted. He was kept alive by the heat of the melting lava.

The Office Job

This happened in the 1800s. The man had applied for a job as a telegraph operator. Among the background noise was a Morse code message saying, "If you understand this, walk into the office." It was a test of the candidates' skill and alertness. He was the only candidate who passed.

The Upset Bird Watcher

The ornithologist was sitting on a plane coming in to land when he saw the rare bird, which was sucked into the jet engine causing the engine to fail and the plane to crash-land.

Damage Control

They strengthened the parts of the aircraft that had not been hit. Antiaircraft fire is random in nature. The returning planes showed damage that had not been fatal. But this sample excludes information from the planes that had not returned and had sustained fatal damage. It was deduced that they had sustained damage on the parts not hit on the returning planes. By adding armor to the planes, overall losses were reduced.

School's Out

She has just celebrated her 105th birthday, but the computer at the local education authority cannot recognize a date of birth that is over 100 years ago. Calculating that she is 5 years old, the computer prints out an automatic instruction to attend school.

The Single Word

The word was "Guilty." I was foreperson of the jury at the woman's trial.

Turned Off

The man was Guglielmo Marconi, the pioneer of radio transmission. When he died in 1937, all the radio stations in the world observed a minute of silence as a mark of respect.

The Last Mail

Both letters were the same weight, a fraction under the weight at which a surcharge was charged. He put the correct postage amount in stamps on each letter. One had a single stamp of the correct value and the other had several stamps adding up to the correct value. When the letters were weighed, the one with more stamps was over the limit and so more stamps were needed.

The Frame Game

The curator is adding inconspicuous identifying marks on a part of the painting hidden from view under the frame, as a safeguard against false claims and ransom demands. If someone claims to have the stolen painting, the curator can ask, "What is the number printed under the frame?" or he can check to quickly ascertain whether, if the painting is stolen and returned, the returned painting is a forgery.

Overdressed

At the airport, George found that he was over the luggage allowance and had to pay for the extra weight. So he took clothes out of his suitaces and wore them, since body weight and clothes worn were not charged extra.

The Knifing

The masked man was a surgeon wearing a surgical mask in the operating room. He saved Sam's life.

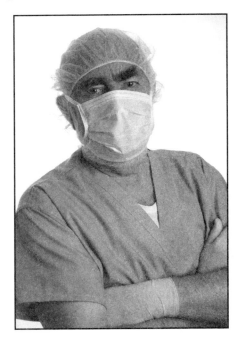

Who's at the Door?

Marjorie worked on weekdays as a gas leak detector. When someone phoned in a suspected gas leak she would visit their house to check for leaks. Gas leak inspectors never ring doorbells in case a spark causes an explosion.

Airport Visitor

The man is a criminal who stands in line with other people at the airport check-in in order to read the luggage tags containing their home addresses. He and his friend then burgle their empty houses.

Hanging Out

The woman lives by the sea and her husband is a smuggler. Her washing is color-coded; certain colors mean "all clear" (there are no police around, so it is safe to come ashore). Other colors mean "danger." The police arrived suddenly so she had to hang out different clothes without any notice.

No Thanks

He was a hunchback. His employment agency found him a position at the University of Notre Dame in South Bend, Indiana, but he did not want to be known as the hunchback of Notre Dame.

Dotty

Banks order automatic teller machines by the thousands and it is cheaper to have them all the same than to have a limited set for drive-in ATMs without the Braille.

Your Turn to Drive

The brothers were Siamese twins, joined at the side. They lived in Birmingham, Alabama. Because they drove on the right-hand side of the road, the steering wheel was on the left-hand side of the car. The brother who sat on the left always drove. When they were in London, England, the other drove because the steering wheel was on the right-hand side of the car.

Coming Up for Air

The girl filled the jar with water at the school. When she reached the appropriate point at the city center she poured all the water out. What replaced it was a true sample of the surrounding air.

Nuts Away!

The boy suggested that the man take one wheel nut off each of the other three wheels in order to attach the fourth wheel. Once he had done this, the man could safely drive to the nearest garage with each wheel firmly attached by three nuts.

The Golf Pro

One of the most important tasks for the golf club professional is giving lessons. Most players are right-handed. They can stand opposite a left-handed teacher and watch and copy him more easily. It is just like looking in a mirror, so it makes learning the correct style of swing much easier.

Flat Tire

The lecturer separated the four students, so that they were not together in the room, and asked each to write down which of the four wheels of the car had suffered the puncture. Of course they did not all say the same wheel. (The chances of them all picking the same wheel are 1 in 4×4×4, i.e., 1 in 64.)

Bottled Fruit

The fruit is grown in the bottle. The bottle is tied onto the branch shortly after the fruit starts to form.

The Village Idiot

The so-called village idiot was smart enough to realize that as long as he kept choosing the 50-cent piece, people would keep offering him the choice. If he once took the $5 bill, the stream of coins would stop rolling in.

Hand in Glove

The manufacturer sent 5,000 right-hand gloves to Miami and 5,000 left-hand gloves to New York. He refused to pay the duty on them so both sets of gloves were impounded. Since nobody claimed them, both lots were subsequently sold off at auction. They went for a very low price (who wants 5,000 left-hand gloves?). Naturally, it was the clever Frenchman who won with a very low bid at each auction.

The Fallen Sign

The man knew the name of the town he had left that morning. So he replaced the sign so that it correctly named the direction he had come from. It would then be correct for all the other directions.

The Cellar Door

When the girl opened the cellar door she saw the living room and, through its windows, the garden. She had never seen these before because her parents had kept her all her life in the cellar.

The Lake Problem

You pour into the lake a known quantity of a concentrated chemical or vegetable dye. After allowing some time for the harmless chemical to disperse, you take samples of the water in several places. The more diluted the solution the greater the volume of water in the lake. Precise analysis of the concentration of chemicals in the samples would give a good estimate of the water volume of the lake.

Albatross Soup

Years earlier, the man had been shipwrecked and ended up on a deserted island with his son and a friend. The man had gotten very ill, and his son had died. The friend fed the man what he claimed was albatross soup, but it was really human soup made with his son. Eating the meat helped the man to survive until a rescue ship came. When he ate the albatross soup in the restaurant, he realized that the taste was nothing like what he'd had on the island. Once he understood that he had eaten his son, he couldn't live with himself and committed suicide.

Traffic Offense

The man was a Samoan motorist who drove to work on the left side of the road as he had for the previous 20 years. Unfortunately for him, it was on the day that Samoa changed over to driving on the right-hand side of the road.

Meeting and Greeting

The woman's hand had just been cut off in an accident, and she was hurrying to the hospital carrying it packed in ice in her handbag.

Garment for Rent

The man was going into a mine with many passages. He unraveled the sweater in order to leave a trail of thread that would allow him to trace his path back out of the maze.

Bad Loser

The man was playing in a chess competition. After losing a game of chess to a computer, the man shot his opponent.

The Unsanitary Janitor

At a school for teenage girls, there had been a problem. The girls applied lipstick and then kissed the mirror on the bathroom wall to check to see if their lipstick was applied evenly. The headmistress called in all the girls and showed them how the caretaker cleaned the mirror. He deliberately dipped his mop in the toilet first. From then on, none of the girls kissed the mirror.

The Man in the Elevator

The man is a little person. He can reach the button in the elevator for the first floor, but he cannot reach the button for the tenth floor. The seventh floor button is the highest he can reach.

The Men in the Hotel

Mr. Jones could not sleep because Mr. Smith was snoring. His phone call awoke Mr. Smith and stopped him snoring long enough for Mr. Jones to get to sleep.

Happy or Sad

It was the final round of the Miss World beauty pageant. The winner was crying with happiness. The disappointed runners-up smiled because everyone was watching them and they were expected to look happy and radiant.

Trouble With Sons

They were two of a set of triplets!

The Miller's Daughter

Her best course of action is to take a stone from the bag and immediately drop it on the path. She can then say: "I cannot bear to reveal my own fate. We can work out the color of the stone I selected by looking at the one that is left. If that is black, I must have selected the white stone."

Water and Wine

They are both equally contaminated. The water contains exactly as much wine as the wine contains water. The most elegant proof for this celebrated little puzzle is as follows: It does not matter how many transfers are made between the glasses or whether the contents are stirred. Provided that the volumes in the two glasses are equal, then any water not in the water glass must be in the wine; there is nowhere else it can be. The wine that it has replaced must be in the water glass. The water glass therefore contains as much wine as the wine contains water.

Old Mrs. Jackson

Old Mrs. Jackson acted as a witness to a document that both the Joneses signed.

Stuck Tight

The little girl suggested that the driver let some air out of the truck's tires. He let out enough to lower the truck by the small amount required to let it pass under the bridge.

Coming Home

The puzzle depends on the reader making the false assumption that the man was coming home at night. He was returning home in bright sunlight, so anyone could have seen him.

Push That Car

He was playing Monopoly.

Woman on the Bridge

The woman waited until the sentry went into his hut. She then sneaked onto the bridge and walked towards the Swiss border. She walked for nearly three minutes, then she turned around and started to walk back towards Germany. The guard came out and saw her. When she reached him he saw that she had no authority to enter Germany, and he therefore ordered her to go back—to Switzerland!

School Friend

Joe's old school friend was a woman named Louise.

The Two Barbers

The traveler deduced, correctly, that since there were only two barbers in the town, each must cut the other's hair. Therefore, the smart barber cut the scruffy barber's hair untidily. The scruffy barber gave the smart barber his tidy haircut. The traveler therefore chose the scruffy barber as the one who would give the best haircut.

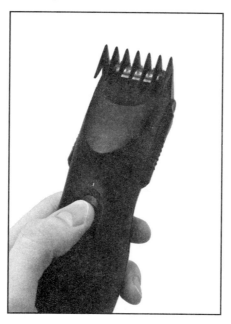

The Plane Hijacker

The hijacker asked for two parachutes (it is believed) in order to deceive the authorities into thinking that he intended to take a hostage. They therefore gave him two good parachutes. Had he asked for one only, they would have known it was for him and could have given him a dud parachute with a tear in it. By asking for two, he eliminated that risk. Once he knew he had two good parachutes, either would do for his escape.

The Hunter and the Bear

The North Pole is one place this can happen. However, it is not the only answer. The other points all lie close to the South Pole.

Any point one mile due north of a particular circle around the Earth with a circumference of exactly one mile will meet the conditions. The circle lies approximately 0.16 miles north of the South Pole.

Starting one mile north of this circle, you could walk one mile south, one mile east (or west), which would take you exactly around the Earth to the same point, and then one mile north, which would bring you back to your original starting point.

Similarly, any point one mile due north of a circle of circumference 0.5 miles, 0.25 miles, or 0.125 miles, etc., would work equally. There are indeed an infinite number of points all near the South Pole that would satisfy the requirements fo the problem.

In any event, the bear would still be white, because only polar bears could survive such cold.

The Arm of the Postal Service

The three men had been together on a flying mission in the Pacific. Their plane had come down and they were adrift for many days in a dinghy. They had had some water but no food and were gradually starving to death. Eventually, out of desperation, they agreed to amputate their left arms in order to eat them. They swore a solemn oath that each would have his left arm cut off. One of the three was a doctor and he amputated the arms of one and then later of the other of his colleagues. Just before his turn came, they were rescued. However, his oath was still binding and he later had to have his arm amputated and sent to his colleagues for them to see that the oath had been kept.

The Book
She was returning an overdue library book.

Mountains Ahead
The plane is sitting on the ground at the airport in Denver, Colorado.

River Problem
First the man took the duck across, then he came back and took the fox over. He left the fox on the far side of the river and returned with the duck. He then left the duck on the near side and took the corn over. Then he returned and took the duck across.

The Seven-Year Itch
The woman had been shipwrecked. She found a pirate's treasure but was not rescued for seven years.

The Follower

He had seen a man hide in the back of the woman's car as she paid at the gasoline station. He followed her to warn her and was pleased to see her pull into the police station.

The Dog Choker

The vet found two human fingers in the dog's throat. They belonged to a burglar. The vet feared that the burglar was still in the house, afraid of the dog and hiding in a closet.

The Elder Twin

At the time she went into labor, the twins' mother was traveling from Guam to Hawaii. The older twin, Terry, was born on March 1. Shortly afterwards, the mother crossed the International Date Line and Kerry, the younger twin, was born. The date was February 28. In leap years, the younger twin's birthday is two days before the older twin's, since February 28 is two days before March 1.

The Key

The man's wife was a habitual sleepwalker. She had previously unlocked the front door (which needed a key to unlock the door from inside) in her sleep and walked out into the road. He placed the key in the bucket of cold water so that, if she reached into the water to get it, the cold sensation would wake her.

A Good Night's Sleep

The man was deaf. He had to get up early for an important meeting and he was so worried about oversleeping that he could not get to sleep. After opening the curtains, however, he knew that the sunlight would wake him up, so he was no longer worried and fell asleep easily.

A Puzzling Attack

They had been trying to solve a lateral thinking problem—this one, in fact. When the one posing the problem revealed the answer, the others beat him up. (In setting this puzzle, always describe the group and the problem poser in terms of the number of men and women in your own group.)

Also Available

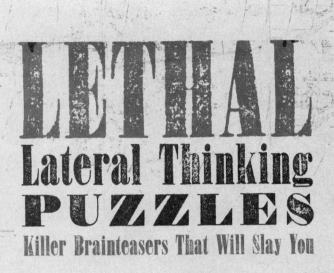

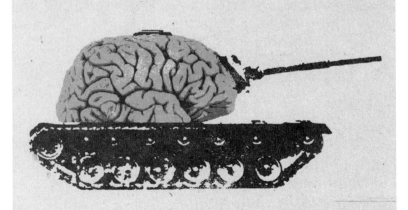

LETHAL
Lateral Thinking
PUZZLES
Killer Brainteasers That Will Slay You

Paul Sloane & Des MacHale